Planner Belongs To:

Bucket List

Date Completed

What I Want To Do:

BUCKET LIST ITEM: #

THOUGHTS & REFLECTIONS

Bucket List

Date Completed

BUCKET LIST ITEM: #

THOUGHTS & REFLECTIONS

Bucket List

Date Completed

What I Want To Do:

BUCKET LIST ITEM: #

THOUGHTS & REFLECTIONS

Bucket List

Date Completed

What I Want To Do:

BUCKET LIST ITEM: #

THOUGHTS & REFLECTIONS

Bucket List

Date Completed

What I Want To Do:

BUCKET LIST ITEM: #

THOUGHTS & REFLECTIONS

Bucket List

Date Completed

What I Want To Do:

BUCKET LIST ITEM: #

THOUGHTS & REFLECTIONS

Bucket List

Date Completed

BUCKET LIST ITEM: #

What I Want To Do:

THOUGHTS & REFLECTIONS

Bucket List

Date Completed

What I Want To Do:

BUCKET LIST ITEM: #

THOUGHTS & REFLECTIONS

Bucket List

Date Completed

What I Want To Do:

BUCKET LIST ITEM: #

THOUGHTS & REFLECTIONS

Bucket List

Date Completed

What I Want To Do:

BUCKET LIST ITEM: #

THOUGHTS & REFLECTIONS

Bucket List

Date Completed [   ]

What I Want To Do:

BUCKET LIST ITEM: #

THOUGHTS & REFLECTIONS

Bucket List

Date Completed [ ]

What I Want To Do:

BUCKET LIST ITEM: #

THOUGHTS & REFLECTIONS

Bucket List

Date Completed

What I Want To Do:

BUCKET LIST ITEM: #

THOUGHTS & REFLECTIONS

Bucket List

Date Completed

What I Want To Do:

BUCKET LIST ITEM: #

THOUGHTS & REFLECTIONS

Bucket List

Date Completed

What I Want To Do:

BUCKET LIST ITEM: #

THOUGHTS & REFLECTIONS

Bucket List

Date Completed

What I Want To Do:

BUCKET LIST ITEM: #

THOUGHTS & REFLECTIONS

Bucket List

Date Completed

What I Want To Do:

BUCKET LIST ITEM: #

THOUGHTS & REFLECTIONS

Bucket List

Date Completed

What I Want To Do:

BUCKET LIST ITEM: #

THOUGHTS & REFLECTIONS

Bucket List

Date Completed

What I Want To Do:

BUCKET LIST ITEM: #

THOUGHTS & REFLECTIONS

Bucket List

Date Completed

What I Want To Do:

BUCKET LIST ITEM: #

THOUGHTS & REFLECTIONS

Bucket List

Date Completed

What I Want To Do:

BUCKET LIST ITEM: #

THOUGHTS & REFLECTIONS

Bucket List

Date Completed

What I Want To Do:

BUCKET LIST ITEM: #

THOUGHTS & REFLECTIONS

Bucket List

Date Completed

What I Want To Do:

BUCKET LIST ITEM: #

THOUGHTS & REFLECTIONS

Bucket List

Date Completed

BUCKET LIST ITEM: #

THOUGHTS & REFLECTIONS

Bucket List

Date Completed

What I Want To Do:

BUCKET LIST ITEM: #

THOUGHTS & REFLECTIONS

Bucket List

Date Completed

What I Want To Do:

BUCKET LIST ITEM: #

THOUGHTS & REFLECTIONS

Bucket List

Date Completed

What I Want To Do:

BUCKET LIST ITEM: #

THOUGHTS & REFLECTIONS

Bucket List

Date Completed

What I Want To Do:

BUCKET LIST ITEM: #

THOUGHTS & REFLECTIONS

Bucket List

Date Completed

What I Want To Do:

BUCKET LIST ITEM: #

THOUGHTS & REFLECTIONS

Bucket List

Date Completed

What I Want To Do:

BUCKET LIST ITEM: #

THOUGHTS & REFLECTIONS

Bucket List

Date Completed

What I Want To Do:

BUCKET LIST ITEM: #

THOUGHTS & REFLECTIONS

Bucket List

Date Completed

What I Want To Do:

BUCKET LIST ITEM: #

THOUGHTS & REFLECTIONS

Bucket List

Date Completed

What I Want To Do:

BUCKET LIST ITEM: #

THOUGHTS & REFLECTIONS

Bucket List

Date Completed

What I Want To Do:

BUCKET LIST ITEM: #

THOUGHTS & REFLECTIONS

Bucket List

Date Completed

What I Want To Do:

BUCKET LIST ITEM: #

THOUGHTS & REFLECTIONS

Bucket List

Date Completed

What I Want To Do:

BUCKET LIST ITEM: #

THOUGHTS & REFLECTIONS

Bucket List

Date Completed

What I Want To Do:

BUCKET LIST ITEM: #

THOUGHTS & REFLECTIONS

Bucket List

Date Completed

What I Want To Do:

BUCKET LIST ITEM: #

THOUGHTS & REFLECTIONS

Bucket List

Date Completed

What I Want To Do:

BUCKET LIST ITEM: #

THOUGHTS & REFLECTIONS

Bucket List

Date Completed

What I Want To Do:

BUCKET LIST ITEM: #

THOUGHTS & REFLECTIONS

Bucket List

Date Completed

What I Want To Do:

BUCKET LIST ITEM: #

THOUGHTS & REFLECTIONS

Bucket List

Date Completed

What I Want To Do:

BUCKET LIST ITEM: #

THOUGHTS & REFLECTIONS

Bucket List

Date Completed

What I Want To Do:

BUCKET LIST ITEM: #

THOUGHTS & REFLECTIONS

Bucket List

Date Completed

What I Want To Do:

BUCKET LIST ITEM: #

THOUGHTS & REFLECTIONS

Bucket List

Date Completed

What I Want To Do:

BUCKET LIST ITEM: #

THOUGHTS & REFLECTIONS

Bucket List

Date Completed

What I Want To Do:

BUCKET LIST ITEM: #

THOUGHTS & REFLECTIONS

Bucket List

Date Completed

What I Want To Do:

BUCKET LIST ITEM: #

THOUGHTS & REFLECTIONS

Bucket List

Date Completed [   ]

What I Want To Do:

BUCKET LIST ITEM: #

THOUGHTS & REFLECTIONS

Bucket List

Date Completed

BUCKET LIST ITEM: #

THOUGHTS & REFLECTIONS

Bucket List

Date Completed

What I Want To Do:

BUCKET LIST ITEM: #

THOUGHTS & REFLECTIONS

Bucket List

Date Completed

What I Want To Do:

BUCKET LIST ITEM: #

THOUGHTS & REFLECTIONS

Travel Bucket List Tracker

Travel Bucket List

Places I Want To Visit

Travel Bucket List

Places I Want To Visit	

Travel Bucket List

EXPLORING THE WORLD *Checklist*

Date Completed: ⬭

Where: _____

With Who: _____

_____

_____

_____

_____

_____

_____

_____

_____

_____

_____

_____

_____

THOUGHTS & REFLECTIONS

_____

_____

_____

_____

_____

_____

_____

_____

_____

_____

_____

_____

_____

_____

_____

Travel Bucket List

EXPLORING THE WORLD *Checklist*

Date Completed:

Where: _____

With Who: _____

THOUGHTS & REFLECTIONS

Travel Bucket List

EXPLORING THE WORLD *Checklist*

Date Completed:

Where: _____

With Who: _____

THOUGHTS & REFLECTIONS

Travel Bucket List

EXPLORING THE WORLD *Checklist*

Date Completed:

Where: _____

With Who: _____

THOUGHTS & REFLECTIONS

Travel Bucket List

EXPLORING THE WORLD *Checklist*

Date Completed:

Where: _____

With Who: _____

THOUGHTS & REFLECTIONS

Travel Bucket List

EXPLORING THE WORLD *Checklist*

Date Completed: ⬤

Where: _____

With Who: _____

THOUGHTS & REFLECTIONS

Travel Bucket List

EXPLORING THE WORLD *Checklist*

Date Completed:

Where: _____

With Who: _____

_____

_____

_____

_____

_____

_____

_____

THOUGHTS & REFLECTIONS

_____

_____

_____

_____

_____

_____

_____

_____

_____

_____

_____

_____

_____

Travel Bucket List

EXPLORING THE WORLD *Checklist*

Date Completed:

Where: _____

With Who: _____

THOUGHTS & REFLECTIONS

Travel Bucket List

EXPLORING THE WORLD *Checklist*

Date Completed: ◯

Where: _____

With Who: _____

THOUGHTS & REFLECTIONS

Travel Bucket List

EXPLORING THE WORLD *Checklist*

Date Completed: ⬤

Where: _____

With Who: _____

_____
_____
_____
_____
_____
_____
_____
_____
_____
_____

THOUGHTS & REFLECTIONS

_____
_____
_____
_____
_____
_____
_____
_____
_____
_____
_____
_____
_____
_____

Travel Bucket List

EXPLORING THE WORLD *Checklist*

Date Completed: ⬤

Where: _____

With Who: _____

THOUGHTS & REFLECTIONS

Travel Bucket List

EXPLORING THE WORLD *Checklist*

Date Completed:

Where: ....

With Who: ....

THOUGHTS & REFLECTIONS

Travel Bucket List

Places I Want To Visit	

Travel Bucket List

Places I Want To Visit	

Travel Bucket List

EXPLORING THE WORLD *Checklist*

Date Completed:

Where: _____

With Who: _____

THOUGHTS & REFLECTIONS

Travel Bucket List

EXPLORING THE WORLD *Checklist*   *Date Completed:* ◯

Where: _____

With Who: _____

THOUGHTS & REFLECTIONS

Travel Bucket List

EXPLORING THE WORLD *Checklist*

Date Completed:

Where: _____

With Who: _____

THOUGHTS & REFLECTIONS

Travel Bucket List

EXPLORING THE WORLD *Checklist*

Date Completed:

Where: _____

With Who: _____

THOUGHTS & REFLECTIONS

Travel Bucket List

EXPLORING THE WORLD *Checklist*

Date Completed: ⬤

Where: ....

With Who: ....

_____
_____
_____
_____
_____
_____
_____
_____
_____
_____

THOUGHTS & REFLECTIONS

_____
_____
_____
_____
_____
_____
_____
_____
_____
_____
_____
_____
_____
_____

Travel Bucket List

EXPLORING THE WORLD *Checklist*

Date Completed: ◯

Where: _____

With Who: _____

THOUGHTS & REFLECTIONS

Travel Bucket List

EXPLORING THE WORLD *Checklist*

Date Completed:

Where: _____

With Who: _____

THOUGHTS & REFLECTIONS

Travel Bucket List

EXPLORING THE WORLD *Checklist*

Date Completed:

Where: _____

With Who: _____

THOUGHTS & REFLECTIONS

Travel Bucket List

EXPLORING THE WORLD *Checklist*

Date Completed:

Where: ....

With Who: ....

THOUGHTS & REFLECTIONS

Travel Bucket List

EXPLORING THE WORLD *Checklist*

Date Completed:

Where: ....

With Who: ....

THOUGHTS & REFLECTIONS

Travel Bucket List

EXPLORING THE WORLD *Checklist*

Date Completed:

Where: _____

With Who: _____

THOUGHTS & REFLECTIONS

Travel Bucket List

EXPLORING THE WORLD *Checklist*

Date Completed:

Where: _____

With Who: _____

THOUGHTS & REFLECTIONS

Travel Bucket List

Places I Want To Visit

Travel Bucket List

Places I Want To Visit	

Travel Bucket List

EXPLORING THE WORLD *Checklist*

Date Completed:

Where: _____

With Who: _____

THOUGHTS & REFLECTIONS

Travel Bucket List

EXPLORING THE WORLD *Checklist*

Date Completed:

Where: _____

With Who: _____

THOUGHTS & REFLECTIONS

Travel Bucket List

EXPLORING THE WORLD *Checklist*

Date Completed:

Where: _____

With Who: _____

THOUGHTS & REFLECTIONS

Travel Bucket List

EXPLORING THE WORLD *Checklist*

Date Completed:

Where: _____

With Who: _____

THOUGHTS & REFLECTIONS

Travel Bucket List

EXPLORING THE WORLD *Checklist*

Date Completed:

Where: _____

With Who: _____

THOUGHTS & REFLECTIONS

Travel Bucket List

EXPLORING THE WORLD *Checklist*

Date Completed: ◯

Where: _____

With Who: _____

THOUGHTS & REFLECTIONS

Travel Bucket List

EXPLORING THE WORLD *Checklist*

Date Completed:

Where: _____

With Who: _____

THOUGHTS & REFLECTIONS

Travel Bucket List

EXPLORING THE WORLD *Checklist*

Date Completed:

Where: _____

With Who: _____

THOUGHTS & REFLECTIONS

Travel Bucket List

EXPLORING THE WORLD *Checklist*

Date Completed:

Where: _____

With Who: _____

THOUGHTS & REFLECTIONS

Travel Bucket List

EXPLORING THE WORLD *Checklist*

Date Completed: ◯

Where: _____

With Who: _____

THOUGHTS & REFLECTIONS

Travel Bucket List

EXPLORING THE WORLD *Checklist*

Date Completed:

Where: _____

With Who: _____

_____

_____

_____

_____

_____

_____

_____

_____

_____

_____

THOUGHTS & REFLECTIONS

_____

_____

_____

_____

_____

_____

_____

_____

_____

_____

_____

_____

_____

Travel Bucket List

EXPLORING THE WORLD *Checklist*

Date Completed:

Where: _____

With Who: _____

THOUGHTS & REFLECTIONS

Travel Bucket List

Places I Want To Visit

Travel Bucket List

Places I Want To Visit	

Travel Bucket List

EXPLORING THE WORLD *Checklist*

Date Completed:

Where: _____

With Who: _____

THOUGHTS & REFLECTIONS

Travel Bucket List

EXPLORING THE WORLD *Checklist*

Date Completed:

Where: _____

With Who: _____

THOUGHTS & REFLECTIONS

Travel Bucket List

EXPLORING THE WORLD *Checklist*

Date Completed: ◯

Where: _____

With Who: _____

_____

_____

_____

_____

_____

_____

_____

THOUGHTS & REFLECTIONS

_____

_____

_____

_____

_____

_____

_____

_____

_____

_____

_____

_____

Travel Bucket List

EXPLORING THE WORLD *Checklist*

Date Completed: ◯

Where: _____

With Who: _____

THOUGHTS & REFLECTIONS

Travel Bucket List

EXPLORING THE WORLD *Checklist*

Date Completed:

Where: ....

With Who: ....

THOUGHTS & REFLECTIONS

Travel Bucket List

EXPLORING THE WORLD *Checklist*

Date Completed:

Where: _____

With Who: _____

THOUGHTS & REFLECTIONS

Travel Bucket List

EXPLORING THE WORLD *Checklist*

Date Completed:

Where: _____

With Who: _____

THOUGHTS & REFLECTIONS

Travel Bucket List

EXPLORING THE WORLD *Checklist*

Date Completed:

Where: _____

With Who: _____

THOUGHTS & REFLECTIONS

Travel Bucket List

EXPLORING THE WORLD *Checklist*

Date Completed:

Where: _____

With Who: _____

THOUGHTS & REFLECTIONS

Travel Bucket List

EXPLORING THE WORLD *Checklist*

Date Completed:

Where: ....

With Who: ....

THOUGHTS & REFLECTIONS

Travel Bucket List

EXPLORING THE WORLD *Checklist*

Date Completed: ◯

Where: ....

With Who: ....

THOUGHTS & REFLECTIONS

Travel Bucket List

EXPLORING THE WORLD *Checklist*

Date Completed:

Where:

With Who:

THOUGHTS & REFLECTIONS

Travel Bucket List

EXPLORING THE WORLD *Checklist*

Date Completed:

Where: _____

With Who: _____

THOUGHTS & REFLECTIONS

Travel Bucket List

EXPLORING THE WORLD *Checklist*

Date Completed:

Where:

With Who:

THOUGHTS & REFLECTIONS

Travel Bucket List

EXPLORING THE WORLD *Checklist*

Date Completed: ⬤

Where: ....

With Who: ....

THOUGHTS & REFLECTIONS

Travel Bucket List

EXPLORING THE WORLD *Checklist*

Date Completed:

Where: _____

With Who: _____

_____
_____
_____
_____
_____
_____
_____
_____
_____

THOUGHTS & REFLECTIONS

_____
_____
_____
_____
_____
_____
_____
_____
_____
_____
_____
_____

Travel Bucket List

EXPLORING THE WORLD *Checklist*

Date Completed:

Where:

With Who:

THOUGHTS & REFLECTIONS

Travel Bucket List

EXPLORING THE WORLD *Checklist*

Date Completed:

Where: _____

With Who: _____

THOUGHTS & REFLECTIONS

Travel Bucket List

EXPLORING THE WORLD *Checklist*

Date Completed:

Where: _____

With Who: _____

THOUGHTS & REFLECTIONS

Travel Bucket List

EXPLORING THE WORLD *Checklist*

Date Completed: ⬤

Where: _____

With Who: _____

THOUGHTS & REFLECTIONS

Travel Bucket List

EXPLORING THE WORLD *Checklist*

Date Completed: ⬤

Where: _____

With Who: _____

_____

_____

_____

_____

_____

_____

_____

_____

THOUGHTS & REFLECTIONS

_____

_____

_____

_____

_____

_____

_____

_____

_____

_____

_____

_____

_____

Travel Bucket List

EXPLORING THE WORLD *Checklist*

Date Completed:

Where: _____

With Who: _____

THOUGHTS & REFLECTIONS

46516623R00075

Made in the USA
Lexington, KY
28 July 2019